The Heinemann Illustrated Encyclopedia

Volume 5

Hom-Leo

First published in Great Britain by Heinemann Library
Halley Court, Jordan Hill, Oxford OX2 8EJ
a division of Reed Educational and Professional Publishing Ltd.

OXFORD MELBOURNE AUCKLAND
JOHANNESBURG BLANTYRE GABORONE
IBADAN PORTSMOUTH NH (USA) CHICAGO

Series Editors: Rebecca and Stephen Vickers
Author Team: Rob Alcraft, Catherine Chambers, Jim Drake, Fred Martin, Angela Royston, Jane Shuter, Roger Thomas, Rebecca Vickers, Stephen Vickers
Reading Consultant: Betty Root

Photo research by Katharine Smith
Illustration on page 6 by Ray Webb, Oxford Illustrators
Designed and Typeset by Gecko Ltd
Printed in Hong Kong by Wing King Tong

02 01 00 99 98
10 9 8 7 6 5 4 3 2 1

ISBN 0 431 09056 4

British Library Cataloguing in Publication Data.

The Heinemann illustrated encyclopedia
1. Children's encyclopedias and dictionaries
I. Vickers, Rebecca II. Vickers, Stephen, 1951–
032

ISBN 0431090629

Acknowledgements:
Cover: The cover illustration is of a male specimen of *Ornithoptera goliath*, commonly called the Goliath Birdwing. Special thanks to Dr George C. McGavin and the Hope Entomological Collections, Oxford University Museum of Natural History.

J. Allan Cash Ltd: pp4, 10, 12, 13, 14, 15, 20, 21, 22, 24t, 26, 29, 30, 33, 34t, 36, 40, 42. **Ancient Art and Architecture:** p23. Breslich and Foss: p38. **Bridgeman Art Library:** p47b. **BBC Natural History Unit:** Brian Lightfoot – p17t. **Bruce Coleman:** Trevor Barrett – p45t. **Hulton Getty:** pp7t, 16. **The Hutchison Library:** p5; T.E. Clarke – p27; Chris Johnson – p46; Lisa Taylor – p34b. **Jazz Photo Library:** Christian Him – p31t. **Peter Newark:** p47t. **Oxford Scientific Film:** p17b; Alan and Sandy Carey – p28b; Kenneth Day – p39t; Richard Day – p9b; Douglas Faulkner – p25t; MPL Fogden – p19; Frances Furlong – p48t; Frank Huber – p25b; Breck p. Kent – p32t; Renee Lynn – p28t; Tom McHugh – p37t; T.C. Nature – p9t; Peter Parks – p32b; Ralph Rheinhold – p6t; Tui de Roy – p37b; Kjell Sandved – p39b; Richard Shiell – p41b; Victoria Stone – p48b; Philip Tull – p6b. **Redferns:** p31b. **Science Photo Library:** NASA – pp11b, 44t; Philippe Plailly – 44b. **Tony Stone Worldwide:** Cameron Davidson – p11t; Mary Kate Denny – p43. **Trip:** p24b. **Zefa:** p7b.

Welcome to the *Heinemann Illustrated Encyclopedia*

What is an encyclopedia?

An encyclopedia is an information book. It gives the most important facts about a lot of different subjects. This encyclopedia has been specially written for children your age. It covers many of the subjects from school and others you may find interesting.

What is in this encyclopedia?

In this encyclopedia each topic is called an entry. There is one page for every entry. The entries in this encyclopedia are on:

- animals
- plants
- dinosaurs
- countries
- geography
- history
- world religions
- music
- art
- transport
- science
- technology

How to use this encyclopedia

This encyclopedia has eleven books, called volumes. The first ten volumes contain entries. The entries are all in alphabetical order. This means that Volume One starts with entries that begin with the letter 'A' and Volume Ten ends with entries that begin with the letter 'Z'. Volume Eleven is the index volume and has some other interesting information in its Fact Finder section.

Here are two entries, showing you what you can find on a page:

The See also *line tells you where to find other related information.*

This is the letter that the entry starts with.

Fact *boxes give you details about the topic.*

A B C D E F G H I J K L M N O P Q R S T U V W X Y Z

Antelope

See also: Deer, Mammal

An antelope is a mammal with horns and hooves. It looks a bit like a deer. Most antelope live in Africa but some live in Asia and North America.

Antelope families

Female antelope and their young often live together in large groups called herds. The herd moves around in search of food. The females visit a male's territory and mate with him to produce new young. The females have only one baby at a time.

ANTELOPE FACTS

NUMBER OF KINDS	over 100
COLOUR	usually brown or grey
HEIGHT	25 cm to 1.8 m
WEIGHT	6.8–545 kg
STATUS	some endangered
LIFE SPAN	2–5 years
ENEMIES	lions, leopards, wild dogs, wolves, coyotes, people

A male bontebok antelope

FOOD

Antelope eat grass and shrubs during the day. An antelope chews its food twice. It swallows the grass almost whole, then later brings it back up to chew again.

Topi antelope and young listening for danger.

–19–

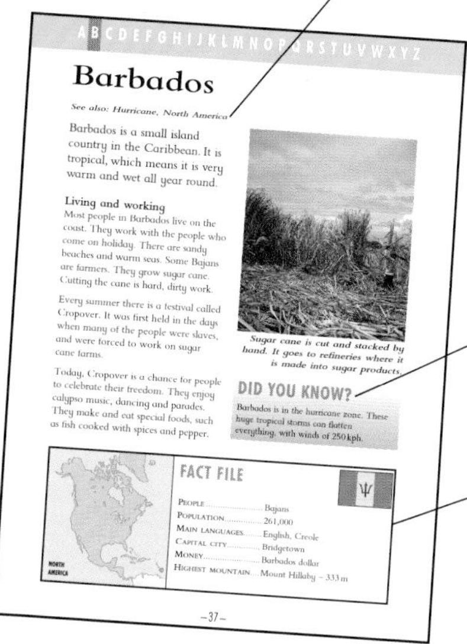
A B C D E F G H I J K L M N O P Q R S T U V W X Y Z

Barbados

See also: Hurricane, North America

Barbados is a small island country in the Caribbean. It is tropical, which means it is very warm and wet all year round.

Living and working

Most people in Barbados live on the coast. They work with the people who come on holiday. There are sandy beaches and warm seas. Some Bajans are farmers. They grow sugar cane. Cutting the cane is hard, dirty work.

Every summer there is a festival called Cropover. It was first held in the days when many of the people were slaves, and were forced to work on sugar cane farms.

Today, Cropover is a chance for people to celebrate their freedom. They enjoy calypso music, dancing and parades. They make and eat special foods, such as fish cooked with spices and pepper.

Sugar cane is cut and stacked by hand. It goes to refineries where it is made into sugar products.

DID YOU KNOW?

Barbados is in the hurricane zone. These huge tropical storms can flatten everything, with winds of 250 kph.

FACT FILE

PEOPLE	Bajans
POPULATION	261,000
MAIN LANGUAGES	English, Creole
CAPITAL CITY	Bridgetown
MONEY	Barbados dollar
HIGHEST MOUNTAIN	Mount Hillaby – 333 m

–37–

Did You Know? *boxes have fun or interesting bits of information.*

The Fact File *tells you important facts and figures.*

Home

See also: Architecture

A home is where someone lives and keeps what they own. Many animals also have homes where they can sleep and look after their young. About half the people in the world live in homes in towns and cities. The other half lives in the country.

This house in Ethiopia is being built with thatch. This is a traditional way of building houses in parts of Africa.

Types of homes

A person's home can be a house, a tent, a houseboat or a flat. Most homes are built to suit the local weather. For example, a house painted white reflects the sun and helps people stay cool in a hot country.

Some people live in cities where there is not much space. Lots of homes can be built in high blocks of flats. These are in New York in the USA.

Families and homes

Some homes are only big enough for a small family. In parts of Africa, a family can include parents, children, aunts, uncles, cousins and grandparents. There are huts inside a walled area called a compound. The family works together and looks after each other.

DID YOU KNOW?

People called nomads move their home from place to place. They live in tents or caravans. Nomads can take their homes with them when they move.

Honduras

See also: North America

Honduras is a country in Central America. There are many mountains and river valleys. There is a long coast in the north and a short coast in the south. The climate is hot and wet, but it is cooler in the mountains.

Living and working

Most of the people live in the mountain valleys and on the coast. There is not much industry in Honduras. Most people work on farms and plantations. Bananas and coffee are grown to be sold to other countries. Farmers also grow maize for people to eat. Tortilla, which are special pancakes made with ground maize, are eaten every day. Hondurans also eat bananas, coconuts and shellfish.

These houses on Bay Island in Honduras are built on stilts with wooden walkways between them.

The music in Honduras is a mixture of Spanish and local Native American styles. There is a special style of local dancing and singing called *garífuna*.

DID YOU KNOW?

Honduras gets its name from the Spanish word that means 'depths'. This is because the Caribbean Sea off the north coast of Honduras is very deep.

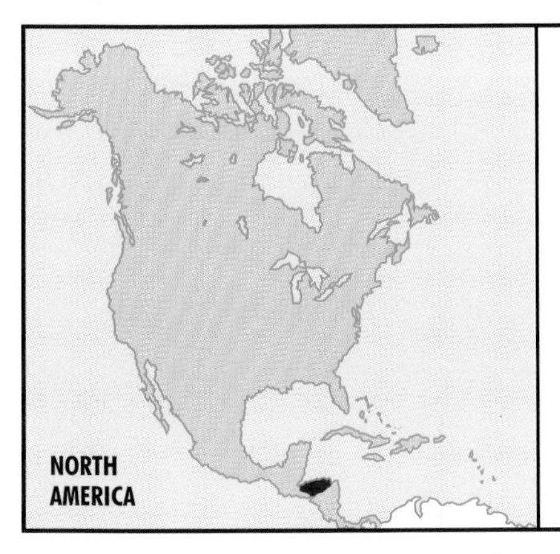

FACT FILE

PEOPLE	Hondurans
POPULATION	5.5 million
MAIN LANGUAGES	Spanish, Native American
CAPITAL CITY	Tegucigalpa
MONEY	Lempira
HIGHEST MOUNTAIN	Mount Celaque – 2800 m
LONGEST RIVER	River Patuca – 320 km

Horse

See also: Mammal, Transport

A horse is a large mammal. Some horses can run fast; others pull heavy loads. Before trains and cars were invented, horses carried people and goods from place to place. Today people ride horses mainly for pleasure.

HORSE FACTS

NUMBER OF KINDS	about 100
COLOUR	shades of brown, black, grey, white
HEIGHT	up to 2 m
WEIGHT	up to 1200 kg
STATUS	common
LIFE SPAN	usually 20–30 years
ENEMIES	mountain lions, wolves

Horse families

An adult male horse is called a stallion and an adult female horse is called a mare. A female horse usually has one baby at a time, called a foal. A young female is called a filly and a young male is called a colt. Horses in the wild live in groups called herds.

Large eyes see well; one eye can look forwards while the other looks backwards

Long tail for flicking away flies

Long, strong legs can run fast or pull heavy loads

Hard hoof protects the horse's foot

An Arabian horse

FOOD

A large horse can eat up to 26 kg of grass or oats and bran every day.

A mare feeds her foal on her milk.

Hovercraft

See also: Transport

A hovercraft is a type of transport that floats on a cushion of air. Hovercraft can move over land or water very quickly.

HOVERCRAFT FIRSTS

First working model	1877
First hovercraft tested	1959
First passenger hovercraft	1962

The first hovercraft

The first hovercraft was a small machine which carried two people. It was built by the British engineer Christopher Cockerell in 1959. A large fan pushed air down, under the machine, to make it float. Later a special skirt was added to keep the cushion of air in place. Then powerful jet engines were added. Hovercraft are now large and fast.

This is Cockerell testing his hovercraft in 1959.

How we use hovercraft

Large hovercraft can carry people and cars. They are fast because they move above the water instead of pushing through it, like ships. They can also travel quickly on land over sand and ice. Hovercraft are used all over the world for short journeys, especially over water. Unfortunately hovercraft engines need cleaning too often for them to travel long distances, such as across oceans. A hovercraft also uses a lot of expensive fuel.

This large hovercraft carries passengers between England and France.

Human body

See also: Blood, Heart

The human body is made up of many parts that all work together.

The human machine

Each of the organs in the human body acts as part of a system. These systems keep the body working. The heart, arteries and veins are part of the circulatory system. They move the blood around the body. The stomach and intestines are part of the digestive system that processes the food that a person eats. The lungs are part of the respiratory (breathing) system.

Healthy systems

All the systems must be working properly for a person to be healthy. Like a complicated machine, all the parts need to help each other. For example, the muscles in the arm and the jaw help a person pick up food and chew it. Then the digestive system breaks food down to find the important things, called nutrients. These are needed by different parts of the body. The circulatory system carries nutrients from the food to the areas in the body where they are needed.

DID YOU KNOW?

Nearly three-quarters of the human body is made up of water.

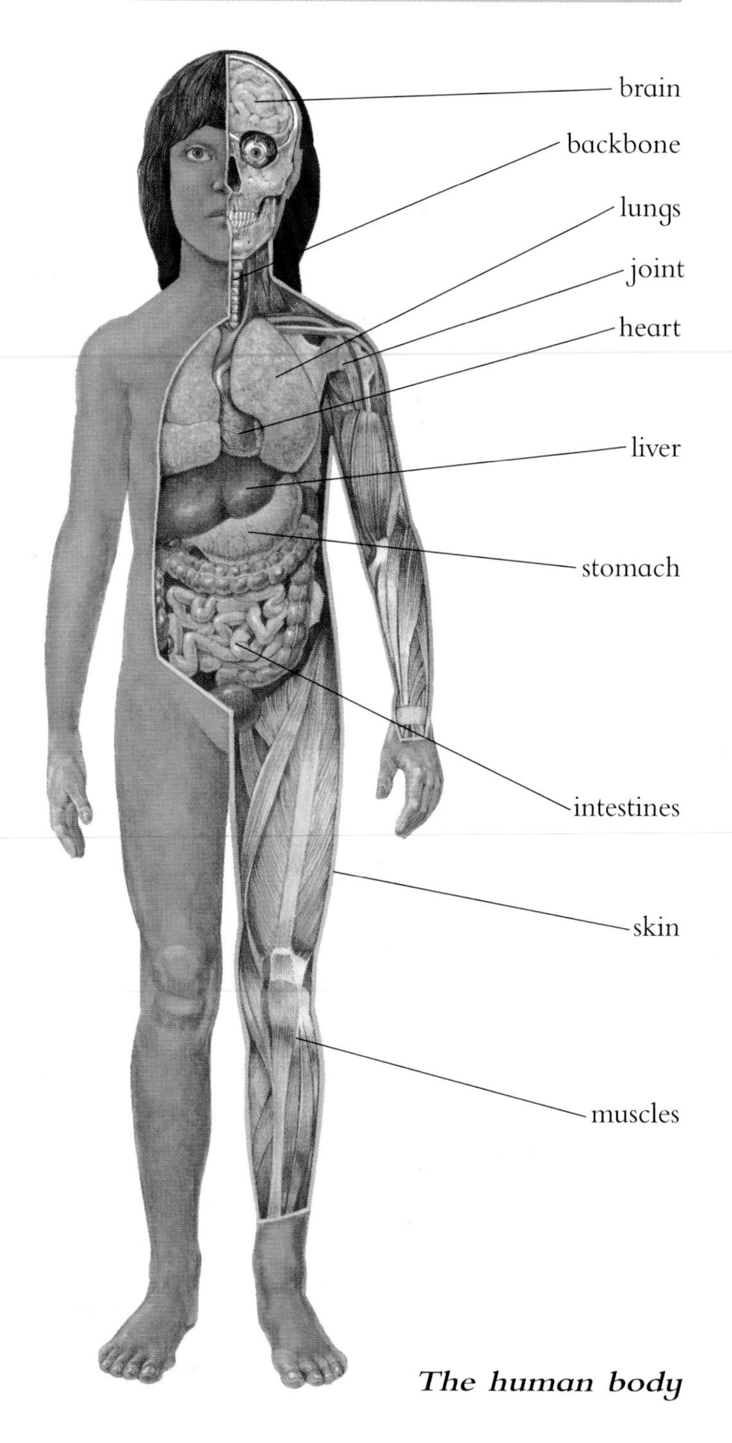

The human body

Hummingbird

See also: Bird, Migration

A hummingbird is a small bird that flaps its wings very fast. It can hover and even fly backwards. Hummingbirds are found only in North and South America. Many hummingbirds migrate to warmer places for the winter. The bee hummingbird is the smallest bird in the world.

HUMMINGBIRD FACTS

NUMBER OF KINDS	334
COLOUR	mostly bright colours
LENGTH	5–15 cm
WEIGHT	2–5 g
STATUS	common
LIFE SPAN	about 5 years
ENEMIES	dragonflies, spiders, frogs, people

Hummingbird families

The male hummingbird attracts the female with a special flying display. The female makes a nest from lichens, bark and spiders' webs, then she lays two eggs. When they hatch she looks after the babies by herself. She feeds them on nectar and insects.

Strong muscles for moving wings very fast, so that it can hover

Long beak for sucking nectar from flowers

Colours help it blend in with the flowers

An Anna's hummingbird

This female ruby-throated hummingbird has covered the outside of her nest with lichen.

FOOD

A hummingbird drinks nectar from flowers and eats small insects.

Hungary

See also: Europe

Hungary is a country in central Europe. Most of the country is lowlands where many crops grow well. There are some mountains in the north-east. Winters are cold and summers are hot.

Budapest is divided into two parts by the River Danube.

Living and working

Over half of the people in Hungary live in large towns and cities. There are factories which make steel, iron, electrical goods and food products.

In the countryside farmers grow grapes, maize, potatoes and sugar beet. Some people keep sheep and beef cattle. The most famous Hungarian dish is a beef stew called goulash. It is made with beef, a spice called paprika and soured cream.

Hungary is a popular place for tourists. The number of visitors per year is more than its population.

DID YOU KNOW?

The capital city of Hungary is Budapest. It used to be two cities, one on each side of a river. Now bridges link Buda and Pest.

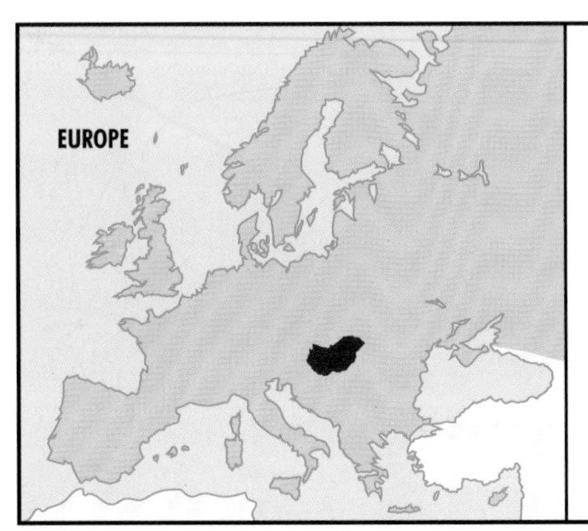

FACT FILE

PEOPLE	Hungarians
POPULATION	10.2 million
MAIN LANGUAGE	Magyar
CAPITAL CITY	Budapest
MONEY	Forint
HIGHEST MOUNTAIN	Kékes – 1015 m
LONGEST RIVER	River Tisza – 1287 km

Hurricane

See also: Climate, Tornado, Weather

A hurricane is a very strong wind. To be called a hurricane, the speed of the wind must reach at least 120 kph. A hurricane can blow down trees, damage buildings and cause huge waves in the sea. In the Pacific Ocean, hurricanes are called typhoons.

This damage in North Carolina in the USA was caused by Hurricane Fran in 1996.

How hurricanes start

Hurricanes begin when warm air rises up over a warm ocean or sea. When more air moves in underneath, air starts spinning around a centre point. This centre point is called the eye of the hurricane.

DID YOU KNOW?

Hurricanes are always given names. Every year, the first hurricane is given a name starting with A, then the next is given a name starting with B, and so on. They are called by male and female names, in turn.

People and hurricanes

People can do things to keep themselves safer during a hurricane. They can cover glass windows in their homes and shops with boards, then go to a hurricane shelter. If they can, they can move away from the area until the hurricane is over.

This picture of Hurricane Fran was taken from a satellite. The eye of the hurricane can be clearly seen.

Iceland

See also: Europe

Iceland is an island to the north-west of Europe. The Atlantic Ocean is south of Iceland and the Arctic Ocean is to the north. It has many volcanoes and glaciers.

Fishing is very important in Iceland. The fish is sold to many other countries.

DID YOU KNOW?

Because of the warm ocean current called the Gulf Stream, Iceland doesn't get as cold in winter as some countries in northern Europe.

Living and working

Nearly all Icelanders live in towns and cities. Some of their homes are heated with water from hot springs. The hot water is also used to keep greenhouses warm for growing fruit and vegetables. The hot springs often squirt out high fountains of boiling water. These are called geysers.

The most important jobs in Iceland are fishing and making other food products from fish. There is not much farming because the soil isn't good enough to grow many crops. Sheep and cattle graze in much of the countryside.

Music is very important in Iceland. Almost everyone plays an instrument.

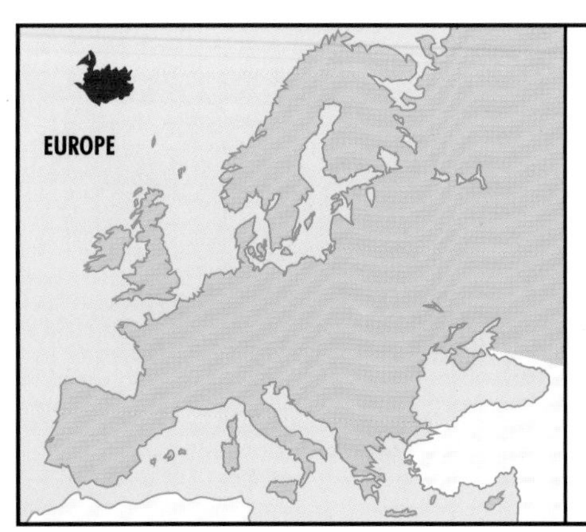

FACT FILE

PEOPLE	Icelanders
POPULATION	266,000
MAIN LANGUAGE	Icelandic
CAPITAL CITY	Reykjavík
MONEY	Icelandic króna
HIGHEST MOUNTAIN	Hvannadalsmukár – 2119 m
LONGEST RIVER	River Thjors – 230 km

Incas

See also: Aztecs, Maya, South America

The Incas were a native people in South America. They ruled part of what is now Chile, Ecuador and Peru about 500 years ago. They began as a small group in about AD 1100, and they took over more and more land and people. By 1525 they ruled about 10 million people.

KEY DATES

1100... The first Incas settle in the Cuzco Valley

1350... Incas begin to take over more land

1439... The city of Cuzco is rebuilt as a capital city

1525... The Inca empire splits into two when its ruler dies

1532... The Spanish arrive and conquer the Incas

What were the Incas like?

The Incas had a king who they treated like a god. There were priests, warriors, traders and ordinary people, mostly farmers. The Incas believed that many gods and goddesses controlled the world, and had to be kept happy. The Incas prayed to them and gave them presents. Sometimes Incas even killed animals and people to give to the gods.

What are the Incas famous for?

The Incas are remembered for their beautiful gold jewellery and their stone roads, cities and temples. They are famous for their way of keeping accounts or records of numbers on complicated knotted strings called *quipu*.

What happened to the Incas?

After 1525 the Inca lands were split between two rulers. Then, in 1532, the Spanish arrived. They used powerful guns and cannon to beat the Incas.

The Inca city of Machu Picchu is now a ruin.

India

See also: Asia

India is a country in the south of Asia. The highest land is the Himalaya Mountains in the north. The River Ganges flows through a wide valley. There are cool, dry winds for part of the year, then warm and wet winds for the rest.

The River Ganges is holy to Hindus. It is used for bathing and washing. People also scatter the ashes of the dead into the water.

Living and working

India's population is the second biggest of any country in the world. Three-quarters of the people live in villages. Most work on farms which grow rice. There are big cities such as Calcutta and Bombay. These cities are very crowded and lots of people are poor. India has factories in the cities making many products.

DID YOU KNOW?

The world religions of Buddhism, Hinduism and Sikhism all started in India.

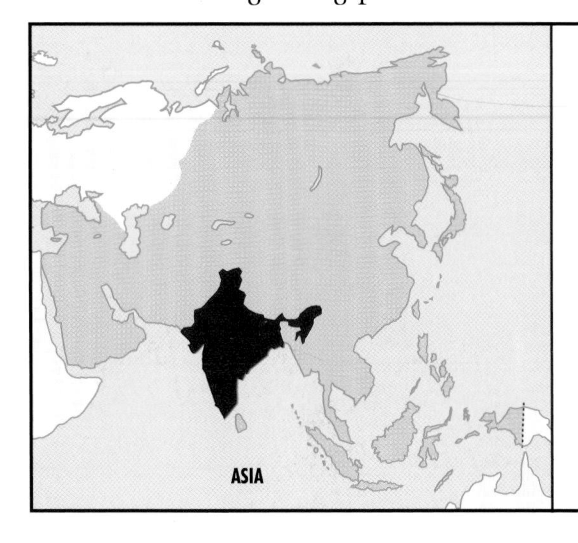

FACT FILE

PEOPLE	Indians
POPULATION	918.6 million
MAIN LANGUAGES	Hindi, English
CAPITAL CITY	New Delhi
LARGEST CITY	Bombay
MONEY	Rupee
HIGHEST MOUNTAIN	Kanchenjunga – 8598 m
LONGEST RIVER	River Ganges – 2506 km

Indonesia

See also: Asia

Indonesia is a country in Asia made up of thousands of islands. There are mountains and active volcanoes on most of the islands. The climate is mostly hot and very wet. Just over half of Indonesia is covered by rainforest.

These village houses in Sumatra in Indonesia are built on stilts to keep cool and dry.

Living and working

About half the people in Indonesia work in farming. Farmers cut steps into steep hillsides to make narrow fields to grow rice, because there isn't much flat land. There are many new factories in Indonesia. Shoes, clothes and other goods are made and sold all over the world.

There are hundreds of different groups of people in Indonesia. They speak different languages and have different customs.

DID YOU KNOW?

The Komodo dragon is the largest lizard in the world. It is only found in Indonesia. It is an endangered species.

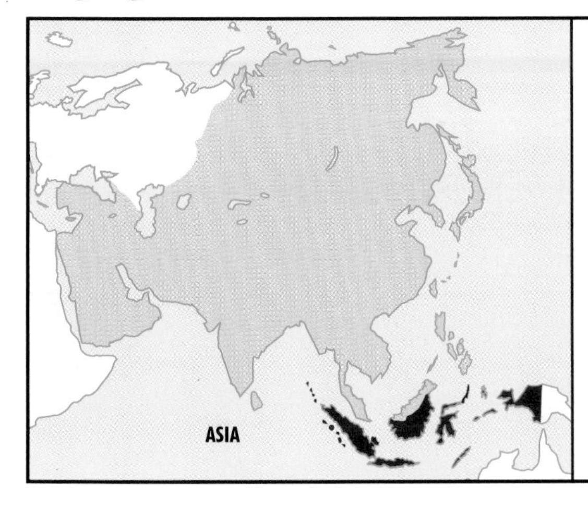

FACT FILE

PEOPLE.................. Indonesians
POPULATION.......... 194.6 million
MAIN LANGUAGE... Bahasa Indonesian
CAPITAL CITY........ Jakarta
MONEY................. Rupiah
HIGHEST MOUNTAIN............. Puncak Jaya – 5029 m
LONGEST RIVER..... River Barito – 885 km

Industrial revolution

See also: United Kingdom

An industrial revolution is what happens when people start making things, like cloth, using machines in factories. Before inventing machines, most people made their living by farming or by making things simply, by hand.

KEY DATES

Different countries have had industrial revolutions at different times in their history.

1750s... Britain became industrialized

1850s... Belgium, France, Germany and the USA became industrialized

1880s... Sweden and Japan became industrialized

1900s... Russia and China became industrialized

1950s... Parts of South America, Asia and Africa became industrialized

The first industrial revolution

The first industrial revolution happened in Britain, from about 1750. Machines were made that could do jobs like spinning and weaving very quickly. At first the machines were powered by water or had to be operated by people. Then coal was used to make steam to drive machines.

The revolution spreads

Other countries found out how Britain was making things using machines. They copied and improved these machines and had their own industrial revolutions.

These machines were used to spin cotton after the industrial revolution in Britain.

Insect

See also: Animal, Invertebrate, Metamorphosis

An insect is a small invertebrate with six legs and a hard covering around its body. Insects are common everywhere on land, in the air and in fresh water.

INSECT FACTS

NUMBER OF KINDS	more than 10 million
COLOUR	often black, brown or green
LENGTH	up to 10 cm
LIFE SPAN	usually less than a year
ENEMIES	birds, spiders, snakes, other animals, people

Insect families

Most insects hatch from eggs laid by an adult female. A young insect is called a larva. The larva can look very different from the adult. When the larva is fully grown, it becomes a pupa. The pupa then changes into an adult. The body of an adult insect has three parts – head, thorax and abdomen. Some insects live together in groups, called communities. Others live alone.

FOOD

Some insects feed on plants. Others eat other animals. An insect either chews or sucks its food.

The green tiger beetle looks just like a green leaf. This helps it hide.

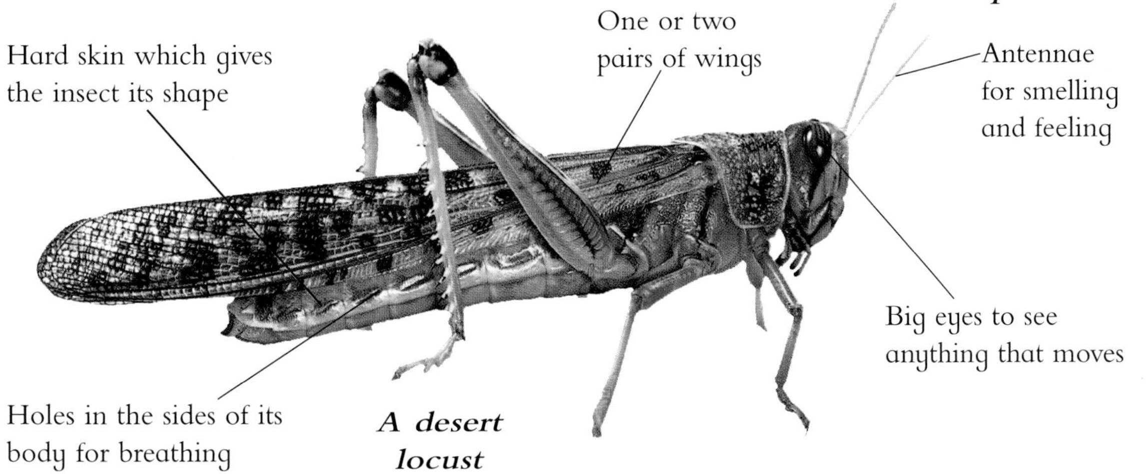

A desert locust

Internet

See also: Communication, Computer, Telephone

The internet is a way of connecting computers together. Computers anywhere in the world can communicate with each other using the internet, so information can be passed between them. The World-Wide Web is part of the internet.

DID YOU KNOW?

E-mail is the short name for electronic mail. The internet can be used, just like letters, to send messages between two computers.

How does the internet work?

The internet started with a few powerful computers. They were connected so that they could pass messages to each other very quickly.

Personal computers (PCs) can be connected to the internet using a modem to send messages along telephone lines. A service provider with a big, powerful computer passes the messages along to other computers. Information can be sent back the same way.

Information is stored in web sites or home pages. These can be about a large range of subjects. Many companies and organizations have their own web sites.

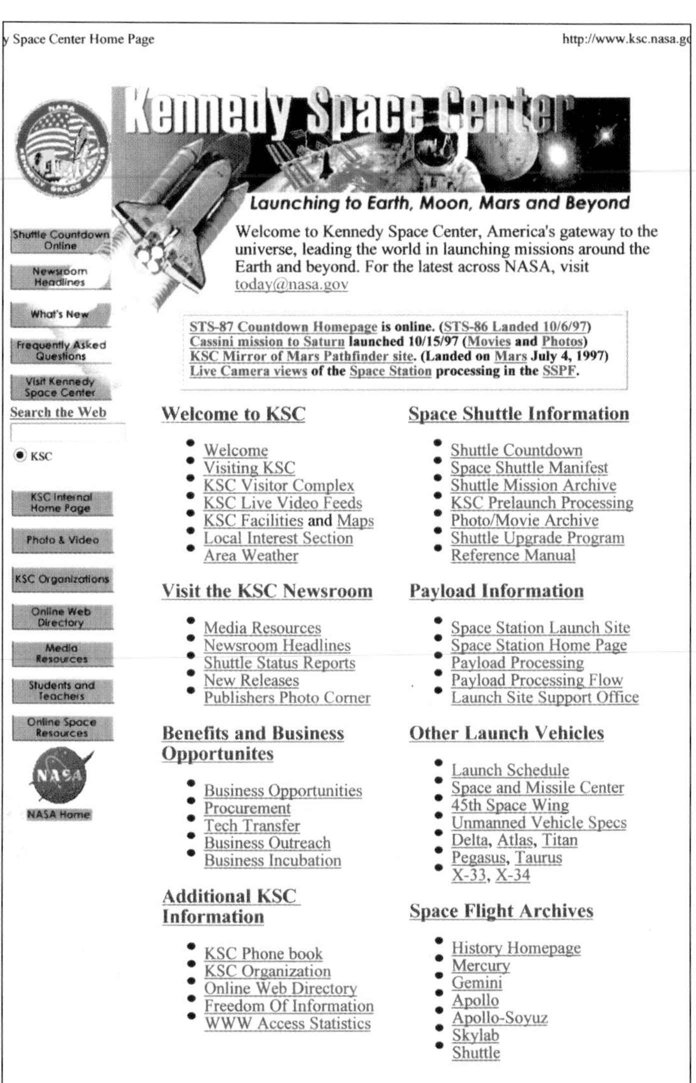

The Kennedy Space Centre web site gives up-to-date information about the United States space programme.

Invertebrate

See also: Crustacean, Insect, Mollusc, Vertebrate

An invertebrate is an animal which has no bones inside its body. Worms, jellyfish, snails, crabs and insects are all invertebrates. Invertebrates are found everywhere in the world.

FOOD

Different invertebrates eat different kinds of plants or animals. The shape of an invertebrate's mouth and body helps it to catch and eat particular kinds of food.

Invertebrate families

Most invertebrates have several stages in their lives. A young invertebrate which hatches out of an egg may not look like the adult. Most invertebrates are male or female, but some are both male and female at the same time.

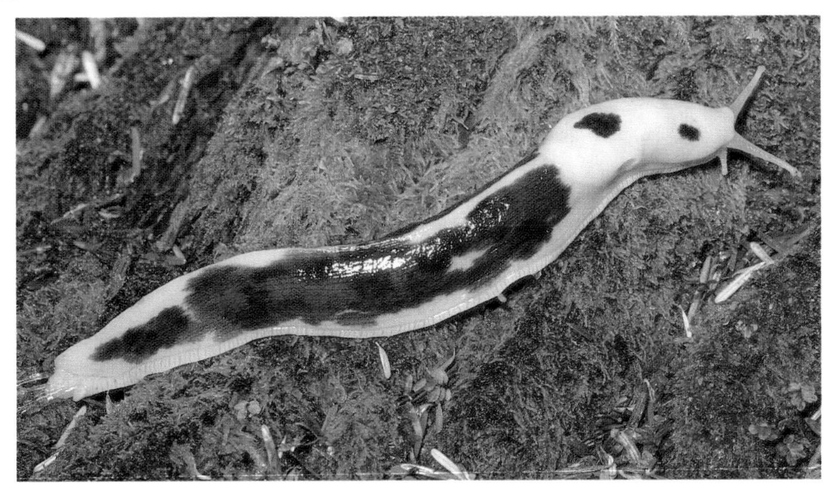

Some invertebrates, like this banana slug, have no shell or hard covering to protect their soft bodies.

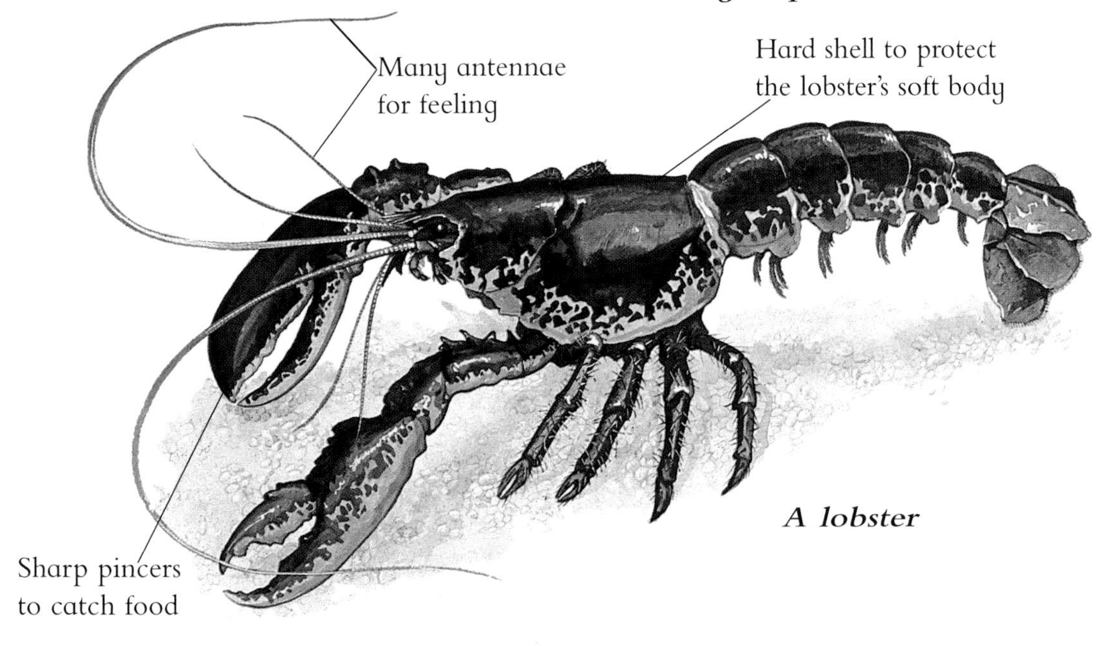

A lobster

Iran

See also: Asia, Islam

Iran is a country in south-west Asia. Most of Iran is high, flat land. There are mountains in the west. Winters in Iran are cold and the summers are much hotter. There is rain in the north but the rest of Iran is usually dry.

DID YOU KNOW?

Some Iranians, mostly women, work making special carpets and rugs. These are called Persian carpets, because Iran used to be called Persia.

Living and working

About one third of Iranians are farmers. The main crops they grow are rice and vegetables. Crops have to be watered because it is so dry. There are many oilfields in Iran. Most of the oil is sold to other countries. Some people work in factories where they use oil to make chemicals.

Some people in the countryside still live in the same way that their ancestors have for hundreds of years. They move with herds of sheep and goats to new grazing areas. These people are called nomads.

Most of the people in Iran are followers of Islam. They have to follow strict laws about how they dress and what they eat and drink.

This prayer tower on a mosque in the city of Isfahan is decorated with mosaic tiles. It is from here that people are called to pray five times a day.

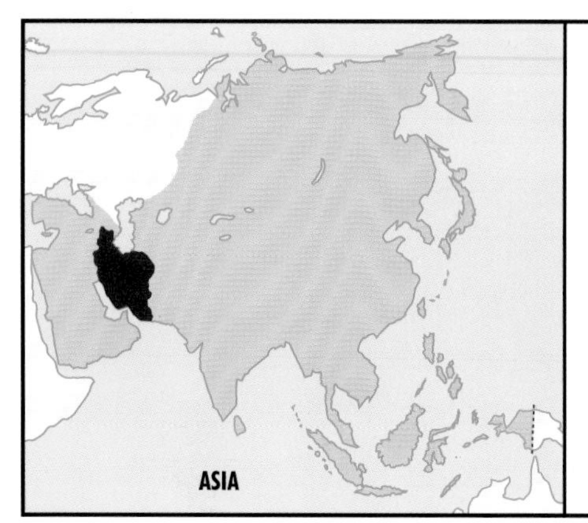

FACT FILE

PEOPLE	Iranians
POPULATION	65.8 million
MAIN LANGUAGE	Farsi (Persian)
CAPITAL CITY	Tehran
MONEY	Rial
HIGHEST MOUNTAIN	Damavand – 5604 m
LONGEST RIVER	River Karun – 725 km

Iraq

See also: Asia

Iraq is a country in south-west Asia. The rivers Tigris and Euphrates flow through flat land in the middle of Iraq. The rivers make marshland as they flow south. There are mountains in the north. Most land in the west is desert. It is wettest in the north.

Street traders sell nuts outside the Golden mosques in the city of Karbila.

Living and working

There is good farmland in Iraq, in the Tigris and Euphrates valleys. About one third of the people are farmers. They grow vegetables and cereals or rear cattle and goats. There are oilfields in Iraq and some of the oil is sold to other countries.

During the 1980s Iraq fought a war with Iran. After this war ended in 1990, Iraq took over the country of Kuwait. Other countries and the United Nations fought against Iraq to help Kuwait. Iraq lost this war, which was called the Gulf War.

DID YOU KNOW?

There are people called Marsh Arabs in southern Iraq who live in floating raft houses made of reeds. The marshes are being drained, so there are not many of these people still living there.

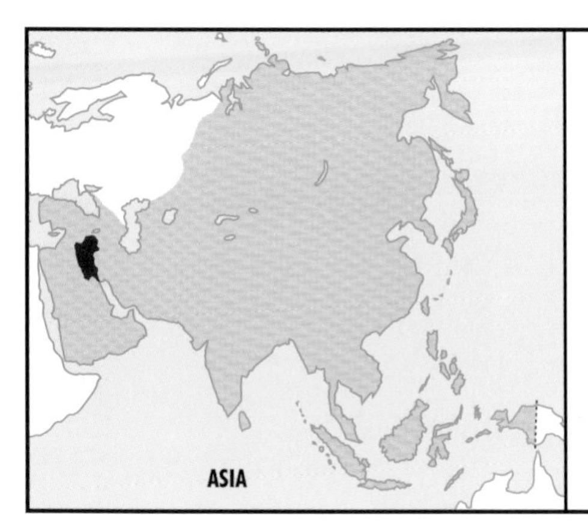

FACT FILE

PEOPLE	Iraqis
POPULATION	19.9 million
MAIN LANGUAGE	Arabic
CAPITAL CITY	Baghdad
MONEY	Iraqi dinar
HIGHEST MOUNTAIN	Huji Ibrahim – 3600 m
LONGEST RIVER	Euphrates – 2720 km

Ireland

See also: Europe, Northern Ireland

The Republic of Ireland is a country in western Europe. It is also called Eire. The centre of Eire is lowland. There are mountains in the south-west and the far north. The weather is usually mild and wet in winter, and cool and wet in summer.

Tourists come to Eire to see the countryside and many kiss the Blarney stone at Blarney Castle. A legend says that this will give you the gift of charming people with what you say.

Living and working

Just over half the people in Eire live in towns and cities. The rest live on farms or in small country towns. More than half the land is used for grazing cattle. Irish cheese and butter are sold abroad. Irish dancing and music are known around the world. Most people in Ireland are Roman Catholic. Gaelic football and hurling are two popular sports.

DID YOU KNOW?

St Patrick's Day on 17 March is the country's main festival. There is a legend that St Patrick drove all the snakes out of Ireland about 1500 years ago.

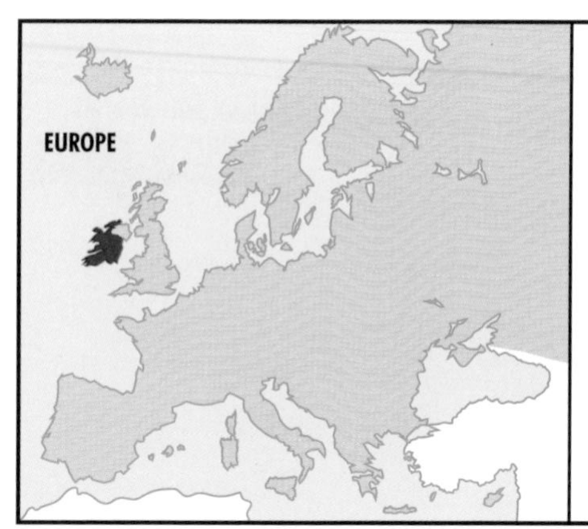

FACT FILE

People	Irish
Population	3.5 million
Main languages	English, Irish Gaelic
Capital city	Dublin
Money	Irish pound
Highest mountain	Carrantuohill – 1041 m
Longest river	River Shannon – 354 km

Iron Age

See also: Bronze Age, Stone Age

The Iron Age is the time in a country's history when tools and weapons are made from iron instead of from stone or bronze.

Why was iron important?

People in different places discovered how to make weapons and tools from iron at different times. Even in the same area, everyone did not start using iron at the same time. First, people had to learn how to get iron out of rocks. Then they had to learn how to make things from the iron.

Tools and weapons made from iron were sharper and stronger than those made from bronze. Also iron does not melt as quickly as bronze, so it is easier to heat and shape while it is soft, but not runny.

What came next?

Iron was used for tools and machines until the 1750s. Then people found that if iron was made very hot and had oxygen blown over it, they got an even stronger metal, called steel. From then, they started making things with steel.

KEY DATES

4000 BC..... People in the Middle East began to use iron from meteoric rocks

1500 BC..... People in the Middle East began to get iron out of rocks by heating them

1000 BC..... People in India and Greece began to use iron

800 BC...... People in Europe began to use iron

400 BC....... People in China began to use iron

AD 1750s... People began to use steel

Iron spear-heads were made to fit onto a wooden shaft. They kept their sharp edges much better than bronze. This spear-head was found in France. It is about 2500 years old.

Islam

Islam is a world religion. Its followers are called Muslims. The religion was started in Arabia, in the Middle East, by Muhammad in AD 622.

Muslims worship on Fridays at a mosque, like this one in the Malaysian capital city, Kuala Lumpur.

Beliefs and teachings

Muslims follow the teachings written in their holy book, the Qur'an. They believe it is the word of God, given to Muhammad by the archangel Gabriel.

One of the teachings of Islam is that there is only one God and that Muhammad is His Prophet. All Muslims must say they believe in God, must pray and must fast (not eat) at certain times. They must also give to the poor and go on a pilgrimage to Makkah. A pilgrimage is a journey to an important religious place. Makkah is the city in Saudi Arabia, where Muhammad was born.

Islam today

There are now about one billion Muslims living all over the world. Most Muslims live in the Middle East, Africa and Asia.

Every year over 2 million Muslims go on pilgrimage to Makkah. They worship and pray together.

DID YOU KNOW?

The Qur'an is written in the Arabic language. The Arabic word for God is Allah, so Muslims call God, Allah.

Island

See also: Coast, Coral, Ocean

An island is an area of land with water all around it. An island can be in a lake, a sea or in an ocean. It can be very large or very small. Greenland is the largest island in the world.

DID YOU KNOW?

Some islands have plants and animals that do not live anywhere else in the world. This is because the sea has cut them off from other places.

How islands are made

Some islands are volcanoes that have pushed up from the bottom of the ocean. The Hawaiian islands in the Pacific Ocean were made like this. Other islands have formed over thousands of years, from living and dead sea animals called coral.

About 10,000 years ago lots of ice melted on Earth. Many areas that had been land were covered with water, and only the high parts were left out of the water. This is how many islands were made.

Only the highest parts of these small islands stick out of the water. The lighter blue shows where there is land very close to the surface under the water.

People and islands

Some islands are too small for anyone to live on. There is no drinking water and not enough land to grow crops. Islands in hot areas are often popular for holidays. They have lots of coast and are good for fishing, watersports and watching wildlife.

This island off Alaska was formed by a volcano. It is still active.

Israel

See also: Asia

Israel is a country in the Middle East. It is mostly lowland. There are some mountains to the east and north. The south is desert. It is hot and dry in the summer and cooler and wetter in the winter.

Jerusalem is the capital city of Israel. This is a view of the old part of the city.

Living and working

Most people in Israel live in towns and cities. Over half the land is used for farming and grazing. Farmers use complicated systems of spraying and pipes to take water to their crops.

Israel only became a country in 1948. It was formed out of part of the area called Palestine. Not everyone in Palestine wanted the new country so there has been fighting and wars ever since 1948. Most of the people living in Israel are Jewish.

DID YOU KNOW?

Jerusalem is a holy city for Jews, Muslims and Christians. Many people make visits to Israel for religious reasons.

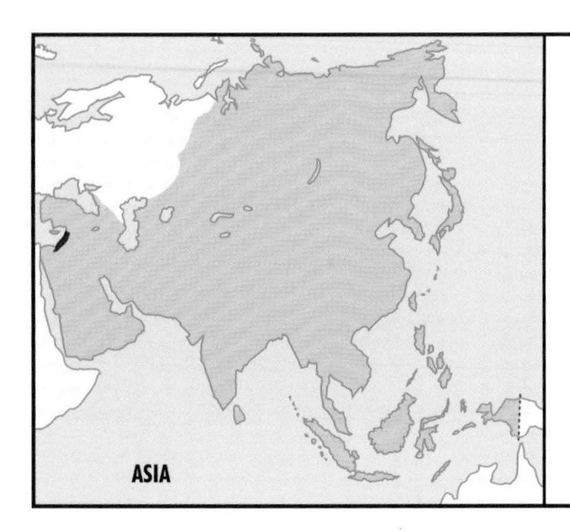

FACT FILE

PEOPLE	Israelis
POPULATION	5.6 million
MAIN LANGUAGES	Hebrew, Arabic
CAPITAL CITY	Jerusalem
MONEY	New sheqel
HIGHEST MOUNTAIN	Har Meron – 1208 m
LONGEST RIVER	River Jordan – 322 km

Italy

See also: Europe, Rome (Ancient)

Italy is a country in the south of Europe. There are mountains in the north and down the centre of the country. The weather is hot and dry in the summer. In winter, it is mild and wet. There are active volcanoes in the south of Italy.

This old tower in Pisa is leaning more and more every year. Scientists hope to support its foundations so it won't lean any further.

Living and working

Italian farmers grow grapes, olives, oranges, wheat and tomatoes. Italian food is famous all over the world. Spaghetti and pizza are two well-known foods from Italy. Italy is also famous for its fashion. There are big fashion shows held in cities like Milan.

The Vatican City in Rome is the centre of the Roman Catholic Church. Many people go to St Peter's Square in the Vatican City to see the Pope.

DID YOU KNOW?

Tourists go to Italy to see the ancient buildings and works of art. Many tourists visit the Italian city of Venice. It is built on mud islands and has canals instead of roads.

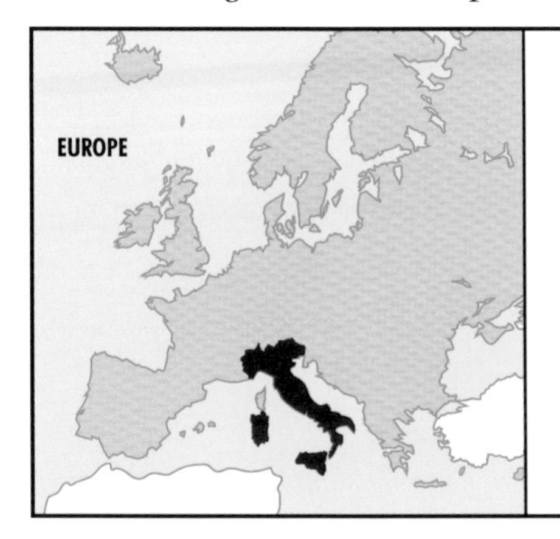

FACT FILE

PEOPLE	Italians
POPULATION	57.2 million
MAIN LANGUAGE	Italian
CAPITAL CITY	Rome
MONEY	Lira
HIGHEST MOUNTAIN	Monte Rosa – 4634 m
LONGEST RIVER	Po River – 650 km

Jaguar

See also: Cat, Leopard

The jaguar is a member of the cat family. It is a mammal. Jaguars live in Central and South America. Jaguars look very similar to leopards, but they are heavier and stronger, with bigger spots. The jaguar can climb trees and swim.

JAGUAR FACTS

NUMBER OF KINDS	8
COLOUR	yellow, with beige and black spots, or totally black
LENGTH	up to 180 cm
HEIGHT	up to 75 cm
WEIGHT	up to 110 kg
STATUS	endangered
LIFE SPAN	about 20 years
ENEMIES	snakes, people

Jaguar families

Male and female jaguars live separately. After mating, the female finds a safe den in which to have her cubs. She normally has from one to four cubs at a time. When they are six months old they leave and hunt on their own.

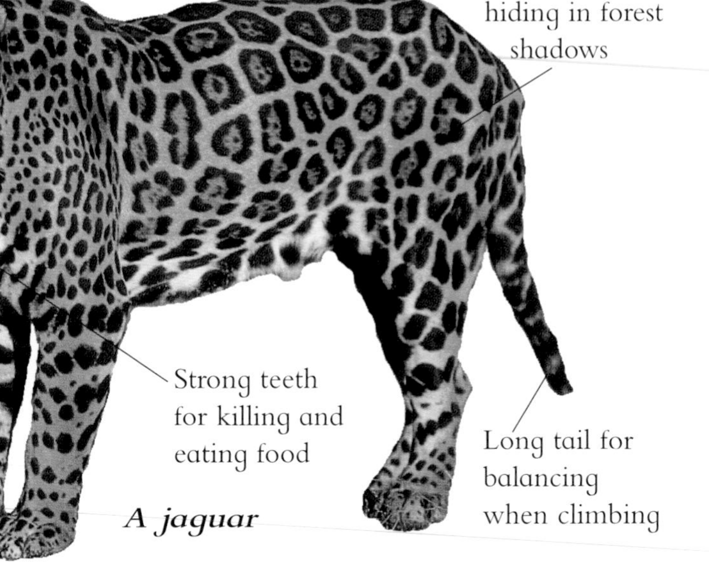

A jaguar

FOOD

A jaguar doesn't need to run far to find food, but hunts by creeping up on animals. It eats big animals such as tapir or deer, as well as small ones like mice.

This young jaguar cub is playing on a fallen tree.

Jamaica

See also: North America

Jamaica is an island in the Caribbean Sea. Most of it is covered with mountains and streams. There are lowlands on the south coast. The climate is tropical and hot all the year round. It is cooler higher in the mountains.

Reggae music began in Jamaica. It developed from a traditional form of Jamaican folk music called mento.

Living and working

About half of the people in Jamaica live in the countryside. For work, many people look after the tourists who go to Jamaica for their holidays.

Sugar cane, bananas, coffee, coconuts and oranges are grown on the farms and plantations. These are mostly sold to other countries. Farmers also grow beans, rice and fruit for local people. Fishermen sell a lot of their catch to hotels and restaurants.

Music is very popular in Jamaica. Some of it, like reggae, is now popular all over the world.

DID YOU KNOW?

The first people who lived on Jamaica were the Arawak Indians. They named the island *Xamayca*, which means 'the land of wood and water'.

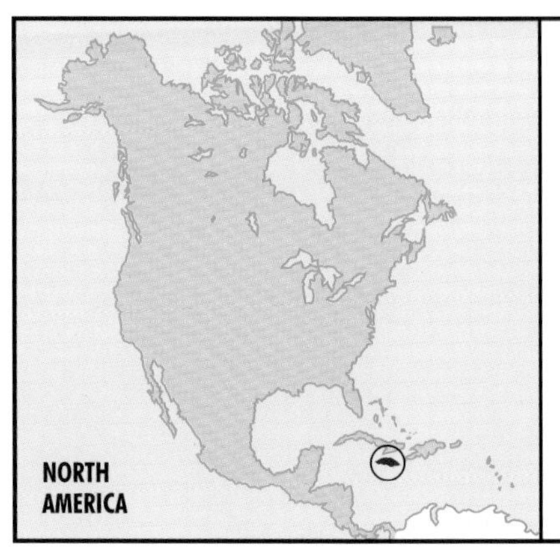

FACT FILE

PEOPLE	Jamaicans
POPULATION	2.4 million
MAIN LANGUAGES	English, Jamaican Creole
CAPITAL CITY	Kingston
MONEY	Jamaican dollar
HIGHEST MOUNTAIN	Blue Mountain Peak – 2256 m
LONGEST RIVER	Black River – 71 km

Japan

See also: Asia, Earthquake

Japan is a country made up of four large islands and many smaller ones. It is in south-east Asia. There are volcanic mountains in the middle of the islands. There are lowlands all around the coasts. The north is cold. The south is hot. There is a lot of rain.

DID YOU KNOW?

Earthquakes are common in Japan. There was a very big earthquake in the city of Kobe, in 1995. Over 5000 people were killed.

Living and working

Most people in Japan live in the cities. Japan has many factories. More electrical goods such as radios, stereos and televisions are made in Japan than in any other country. Japanese ships and cars are sold all over the world. In the countryside farmers grow rice and fruit. Fishing is also important. Rice and fish are often eaten with soy or spicy sauces.

People in Japan still follow many customs from the country's past. There is a special ceremony for serving tea. There are also many rules about how people should greet each other.

Tokyo is one of the world's most expensive cities to live in.

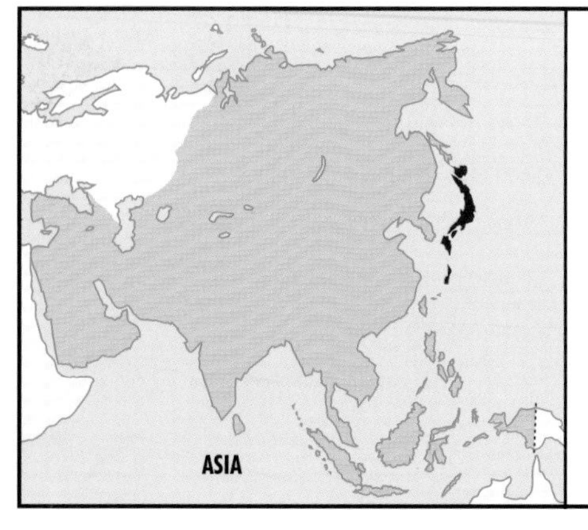

FACT FILE

PEOPLE	Japanese
POPULATION	124.8 million
MAIN LANGUAGE	Japanese
CAPITAL CITY	Tokyo
MONEY	Yen
HIGHEST MOUNTAIN	Mount Fuji – 3776 m
LONGEST RIVER	Shinano – 367 km

Jazz

See also: Music, Musical instruments

Jazz is a form of music started by African-Americans living in the USA about 100 years ago. The important features of jazz are rhythm and improvisation. As the musicians play, they make changes to the tune. Each performance of the same tune can be completely different.

A modern jazz band can use similar instruments to pop groups.

Traditional and modern jazz

Jazz as it started out is now called traditional jazz. It is usually played by a small group of musicians who play drums, bass, piano and sometimes wind instruments such as clarinet, trumpet or trombone. Often a banjo is used to play chords and there may be a singer.

There are many different kinds of jazz today. Many other places in the world, such as Latin America and Africa, now have their own styles of jazz.

Louis Armstrong (1900–71)

Louis Armstrong was born in New Orleans in the USA. He played the trumpet, the piano and the cornet and also sang. Armstrong had many exciting ideas about how to change tunes as he played. When he sang he would often sing sounds instead of words, as if his voice was an instrument. This is called scat singing.

DID YOU KNOW?

The word 'cool' is used today to mean something that you like. It comes from a modern kind of jazz from the 1940s and 1950s, called 'cool jazz'.

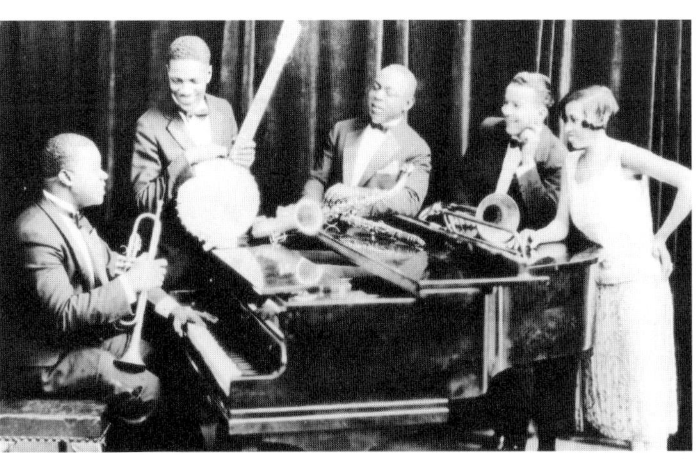

Louis Armstrong sitting at the piano with one of his early groups, the Hot Five.

Jellyfish

See also: Invertebrate, Sea life

A jellyfish is an invertebrate that is made mainly of soft, jelly-like flesh. It is shaped like a bell. Jellyfish are found in all the seas in the world.

Jellyfish families

A jellyfish develops from an egg which hatches into a polyp. The polyp sticks to the seabed and produces buds, which then hatch into tiny jellyfish. These tiny jellyfish grow into large, adult jellyfish.

FOOD

Most jellyfish feed on plankton. This is made up of tiny plants and animals that float in the sea.

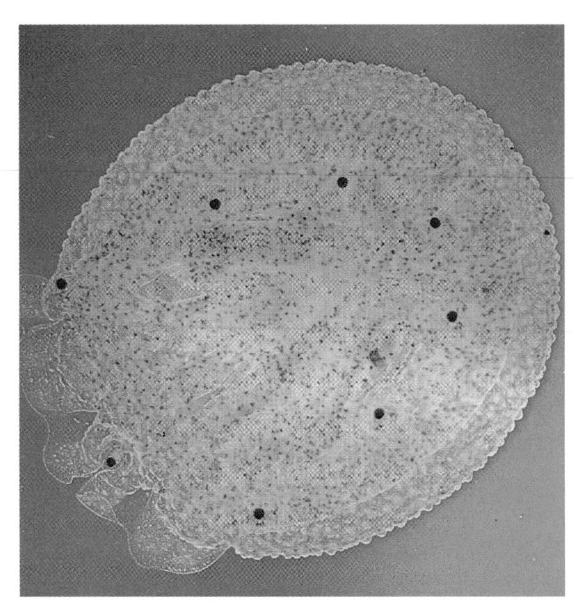

This jellyfish polyp is developing in the sea near the Great Barrier Reef in Australia.

JELLYFISH FACTS

NUMBER OF KINDS	200
COLOUR	clear, pink, orange, blue or other colours
LENGTH	1.5 mm–2 m across
STATUS	common
LIFE SPAN	usually 1–3 months
ENEMIES	fish and other sea animals

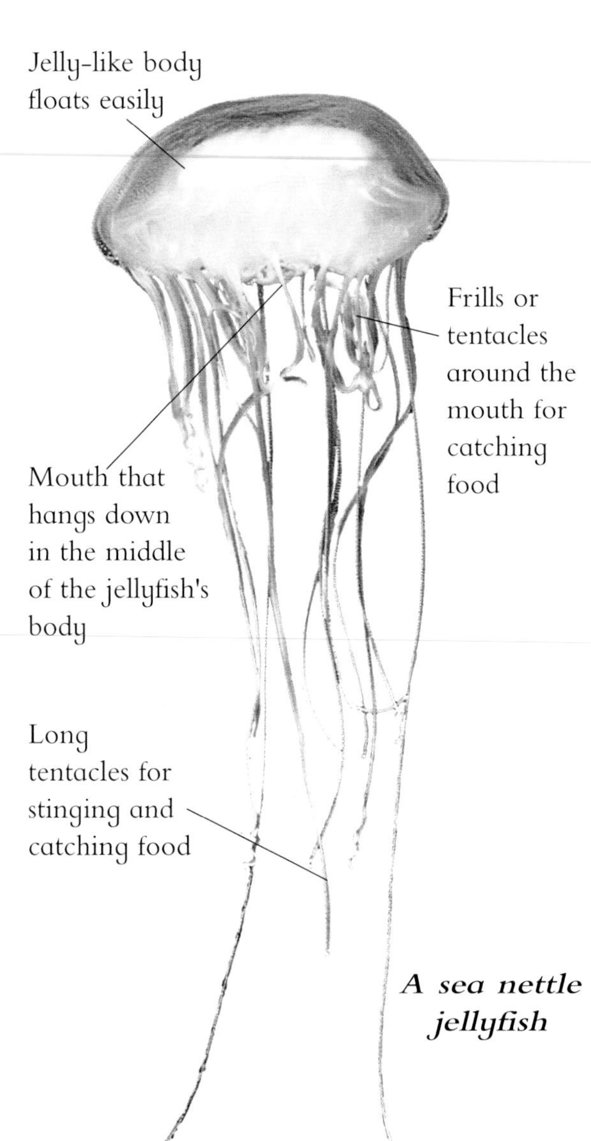

A sea nettle jellyfish

Jordan

See also: Asia

Jordan is a country in the Middle East. Most of it is flat desert. There is a river valley in the west and mountains in the south. The summer is very hot. The winter is cooler with some rain.

These people are wearing traditional clothes. Their headdresses protect them from the sun and can be pulled across the face to keep out sand.

Living and working

Most people in Jordan live in cities and towns. Only a small amount of the land is good enough for farming, but some grains, olives, figs, almonds, grapes, apricots, cucumbers and tomatoes are grown. Some fruits and vegetables are sold to other countries.

In the deserts of Jordan, tribes called the Bedouin live in black tents. They are nomads. This means that they move from place to place with all their belongings.

The people in Jordan are mainly Arabs who follow the religion of Islam. Many of their customs and festivals are to do with their religion.

DID YOU KNOW?

The Dead Sea, which is part of Jordan's border with Israel, is really a big lake. It is nine times more salty than most oceans. Floating in the Dead Sea is very easy.

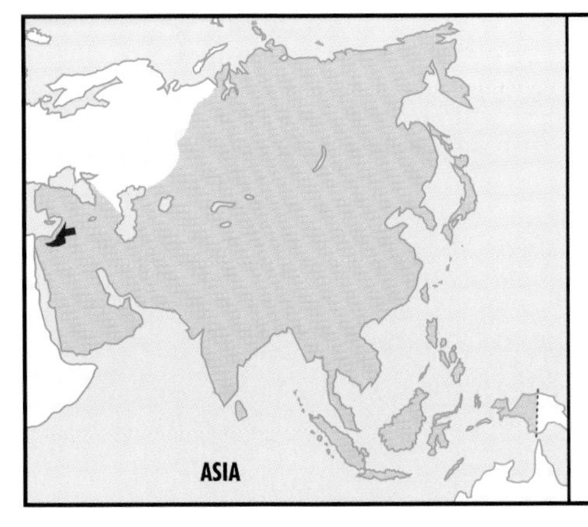

FACT FILE

PEOPLE	Jordanians
POPULATION	5.2 million
MAIN LANGUAGE	Arabic
CAPITAL CITY	Amman
MONEY	Jordanian dinar
HIGHEST MOUNTAIN	at Ma'an – 1500 m
LONGEST RIVER	River Jordan – 322 km

Judaism

See also: Israel, World War II

Judaism is a world religion. Its followers are called Jews. The religion started from the belief in one God. It began in what is now Israel over 3000 years ago.

This is the Western Wall in Jerusalem, in Israel. The wall is all that is left of an old Jewish temple.

Beliefs and teachings

Jews believe that God gave laws, called the Ten Commandments, to Moses. Moses was a leader of the people of Israel. The laws told people how they should live.

One of the most important Jewish holy books is the Torah. It is written in Hebrew, the Jewish language. A Jewish religious leader, called a rabbi, leads services in a building called a synagogue.

This Rabbi is conducting a Jewish wedding ceremony under a special decorated canopy.

Judaism today

There are now about 16 million Jews. Most live in the USA, Israel, Britain and Russia. In Europe, six million Jews were killed during the 1930s and during World War II. The ill-treatment and murder of the Jews during this time is called the Holocaust.

DID YOU KNOW?

Israel was founded in 1948 as a country for Jews. Most of the holy places mentioned in the Torah are in Israel.

Kangaroo

See also: Australia, Mammal, Marsupial

A kangaroo is a large marsupial mammal. 'Marsupial' means that the female has a pouch on her belly, where her baby is carried. Kangaroos live in Australia and some nearby islands.

KANGAROO FACTS

NUMBER OF KINDS	about 50
COLOUR	usually brown or grey
LENGTH	60 cm–3 m
HEIGHT	up to 2 m
WEIGHT	up to 70 kg
STATUS	common
LIFE SPAN	up to 15 years
ENEMIES	wedgetail eagles, dingoes, people

Kangaroo families

A young kangaroo is called a joey. The joey is tiny when it is born. It crawls up the mother's fur and into her pouch. It stays there, until it is about eight months old. Female kangaroos live with their joeys in groups called herds.

A female kangaroo and her joey

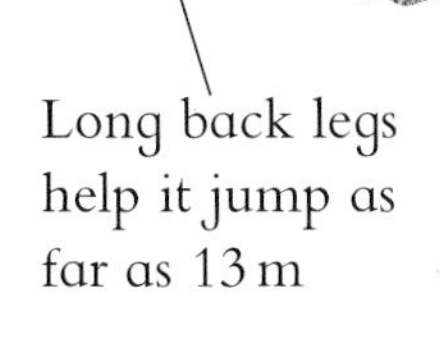

Large ears can turn to catch sounds

Long tail for balancing when jumping, standing or walking

Long back legs help it jump as far as 13 m

Female's pouch shelters and protects the joey until it grows too big to get in and out

When a newborn joey reaches the pouch, it takes one of its mother's teats in its mouth. The teat swells up to lock the joey onto it.

FOOD

In hot weather a kangaroo feeds mainly at dawn and dusk, on grass, leaves and bark. During the day it rests in the shade of a tree.

Kenya

See also: Africa

Kenya is a country in East Africa. There are hot lowland and coast areas in the east. In the west there is higher land, with mountains. The Rift Valley runs through Kenya, from north to south. The north is hot desert. The main wet season is in April and May.

These men of the Samburu tribe are performing a traditional war dance.

Living and working

Most people live in the countryside and work on farms. They raise animals and grow the food they need to eat. Coffee and tea are grown on big farms, to be sold to other countries. The people of Kenya come from 40 different African tribes. The national motto is *Harambee*, which means 'Let's all pull together'.

DID YOU KNOW?

Many wild animals roam in the national parks of Kenya. Tourists go to Kenya on 'camera safaris'. They travel through the parks and take photographs of the animals.

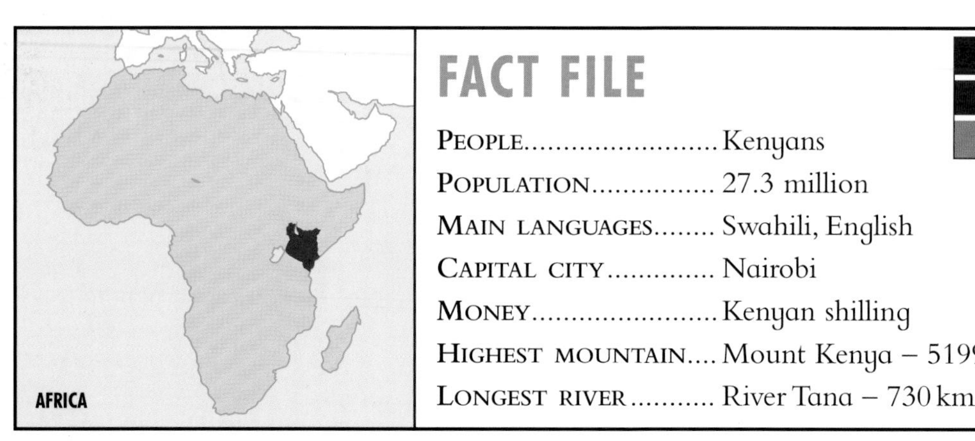

FACT FILE

People	Kenyans
Population	27.3 million
Main languages	Swahili, English
Capital city	Nairobi
Money	Kenyan shilling
Highest mountain	Mount Kenya – 5199 m
Longest river	River Tana – 730 km

Kiwi

See also: Bird, New Zealand

A kiwi is a bird that cannot fly. It lives only in New Zealand. It can run quite fast, and has feathers that look like hairs.

KIWI FACTS

NUMBER OF KINDS... 3
COLOUR.... brownish-grey
HEIGHT...... 35 cm
LENGTH..... 50 cm
WEIGHT..... up to 2.2 kg
STATUS....... common
LIFE SPAN... not known
ENEMIES..... rats, stoats, ferrets

Kiwi families

The female kiwi lays two eggs in a nest hole or in a hollow log. The male sits on the eggs for 11 weeks. This is longer than any other bird. When they hatch, the kiwi chicks have all their feathers and they can see. After a week the chicks leave the nest and go off on their own.

A common kiwi

Long beak for reaching worms

Sensitive nostrils for smelling out food

Strong legs for running and kicking in fights

FOOD

A kiwi sleeps in the daytime and walks around at night looking for insects, worms, berries, fruit and lizards to eat.

This female brown kiwi is with the egg she has just laid. It is very large compared to her size.

Knight

See also: Castle, Middle Ages

A knight was a man who fought on horseback, in Europe in the Middle Ages. Knights fought for the king or queen of their country, or for the most important person in the area where they lived.

What did a knight wear?

Knights wore armour to fight. Armour was made from pieces of metal shaped to fit different parts of the body. It was difficult to hurt a knight who was covered from head to foot in metal. The armour was very heavy, so knights could not move fast. The horses had to be very strong.

A knight fought with a lance. This was a long pole that had a sharp metal piece on the end. Knights also had swords and daggers.

Who could be a knight?

Knights were men from important families. Boys went to live in a knight's home when they were young. They worked as pages, fetching and carrying for the knight and serving his food. As they grew up and learned more, they became squires. Squires were taught how to be knights. When they were fully trained, squires became knights in a special ceremony.

After about AD 1600 people did not need knights to fight any more.

Armour was very complicated. These pictures show all the layers of clothes a knight needed to put on.

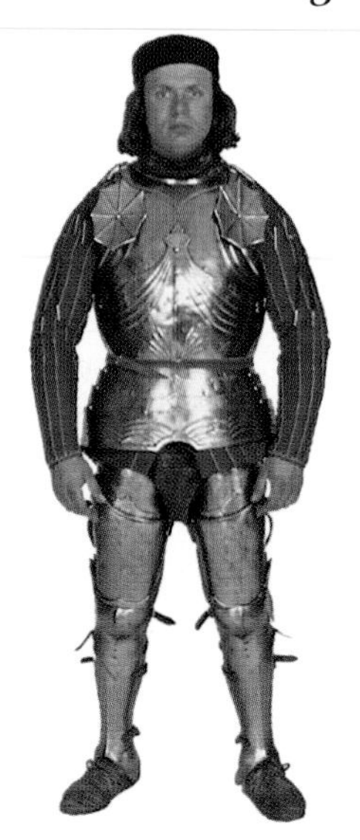

Koala

See also: Australia, Mammal, Marsupial

A koala is a marsupial mammal that looks like a small bear. Females have pouches for their young. Koalas live only in Australia. A koala lives most of its life in the trees. It can walk or swing from tree to tree. A koala never drinks because it gets all the water it needs from the eucalyptus leaves it eats.

Koala families

When a baby koala is born it is only 2 cm long. It is blind and hairless. It must climb through its mother's fur to her pouch, where it lives on her milk. At six months old, the baby leaves the pouch and moves onto its mother's back. She carries it piggyback until it is fully grown.

KOALA FACTS

NUMBER OF KINDS.... 1
COLOUR..... grey and white
LENGTH..... up to 78 cm
WEIGHT..... up to 11.8 kg
STATUS....... common
LIFE SPAN... about 15–20 years
ENEMIES..... People destroy eucalyptus forests.

A koala

A female koala with her baby, eating at night.

FOOD

A koala is a very fussy eater. The only food it will eat is the leaves from twelve kinds of eucalyptus tree. A koala feeds at night. It needs so much food that it has to move from one tree to another to find enough leaves.

Kuwait

See also: Asia, Desert

Kuwait is a country in the Middle East. It is all flat lowland, with a coast in the east. It is mostly very hot desert. From October to March it is slightly cooler. There is very little rain.

These men are building a dhow. This is a traditional Arab sailboat.

Living and working

Nearly everybody in Kuwait lives in cities or towns. Kuwait City is very modern with lots of high-rise buildings. The only big industry in the country is the production of oil and natural gas. There are thousands of oilwells.

No food can be grown in Kuwait, but shrimp and fish are caught in the sea. All other food has to be bought from other countries. Drinking water has to be made by removing the salt from sea water in special factories. This is called desalination.

DID YOU KNOW?

Kuwait is one of the Gulf States. This is the name given to all the countries around the part of the Indian Ocean that is called the Arabian Gulf.

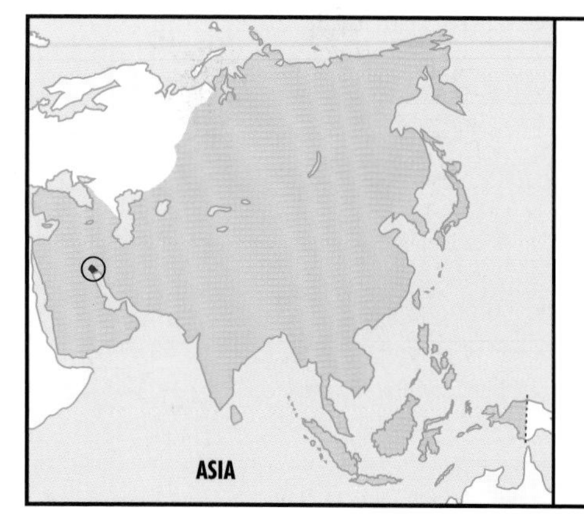

FACT FILE

PEOPLE	Kuwaitis
POPULATION	1.6 million
MAIN LANGUAGE	Arabic
CAPITAL CITY	Kuwait City
MONEY	Kuwaiti dinar
HIGHEST MOUNTAIN	no land above 200 m
LONGEST RIVER	no rivers

Ladybird

See also: Beetle, Insect

A ladybird is a brightly-coloured spotted beetle. This insect is found in most parts of the world, except for very cold places.

LADYBIRD FACTS

NUMBER OF KINDS	5000
COLOUR	brightly coloured with black, yellow or red spots
LENGTH	8–10 mm
STATUS	common
LIFE SPAN	less than a year
ENEMIES	birds, chemical pesticides

Ladybird families

A ladybird starts life as an egg which hatches into a larva. The larva is a grey grub with black, red, blue or green spots. When it is fully grown the larva spins a special covering and forms a pupa. Inside the pupa it changes into an adult ladybird.

Different kinds of ladybird have different numbers and colours of spots

A ladybird

Hard covers to protect the wings underneath

FOOD

A ladybird is a friend to gardeners and farmers because it eats greenfly and other insects which damage plants.

These young ladybirds are gathering together in a swarm.

Lake

See also: River, Valley

A lake is an area of water with land all around it. Some lakes are so big that they are called seas. A very small lake is called a pond.

The Great Salt Lake is in Utah, in the United States.

How lakes are made

About 10,000 years ago, much of the Earth was covered in ice. Deep hollows were made in the ground by sheets of ice. Lakes later formed in these hollows. Some lakes form where the Earth's surface is cracked and has sunk. These cracks are called fault lines.

There is fresh water in most lakes. Rivers with fresh water sometimes flow into lakes and then flow out again. Some lakes, such as the Great Salt Lake, are very salty. This happens because rivers carrying salt from rocks flow into the lakes.

DID YOU KNOW?

The deepest lakes in Africa are along a huge crack called the Great Rift Valley. Water has filled the hollows where the land has sunk.

People and lakes

Lakes are a good way to move goods. Large boats can carry far more goods than trucks or trains. Lakes are also used for fishing, boating and watersports, and are important homes for wildlife. People make special lakes to store water. These are called reservoirs.

Loch Ness, in Scotland, is a lake which has formed along a fault line. It is famous for the monster that some people believe lives there.

Language

See also: Alphabet, Communication

Language is the way that people communicate with each other. People use language to say what they want, think or feel. Animals and human beings use their bodies, sounds and special movements to communicate. Human beings also use the language of spoken and written words. Today, there are about 5000 languages in the world.

Chinese / Japanese	魚
Dutch	VIS
Spanish	PEZ
Greek	ΨAPI
Russian	РЫБА
Finnish	KALA
Swedish	FISK
English	FISH
German	FISCH
Italian	PESCE
French	POISSON
Turkish	BALIK

Here is the word fish in twelve languages. In some languages this word is very similar, but in others it looks completely different.

Language around the world

More people speak Chinese than any other language. Many people also speak English, Hindi, Spanish, French, Russian and Arabic. In Africa there are about 1300 languages. All of them probably grew from four languages, and then changed over time.

English

The English language began to spread around the world about 400 years ago. People took it to other places as they travelled from Britain. Now more than 320 million people speak English. Many also learn it as a second language.

DID YOU KNOW?

Special ways to communicate, called sign language, have been invented for people who have problems with hearing or speech. Using sign language, people use their hands to make symbols or spell out words.

Here sign language is being used by a teacher to read a story to deaf children.

Laser

See also: Bar code, Computer, Light

A laser is a machine that makes a ray of light. Lasers have many different uses. Tiny lasers are used in CD players and cable TV. More powerful lasers are used in medical operations.

DID YOU KNOW?

A hologram is a photo or image made using lasers. Two laser beams are shone from different directions to give views from both sides. When you look at the hologram, you can see the image from different angles.

How do lasers work?

All beams of light carry energy. All of the energy in a laser beam shines in a narrow beam onto a tiny spot. If the laser is powerful this tiny spot will get very hot.

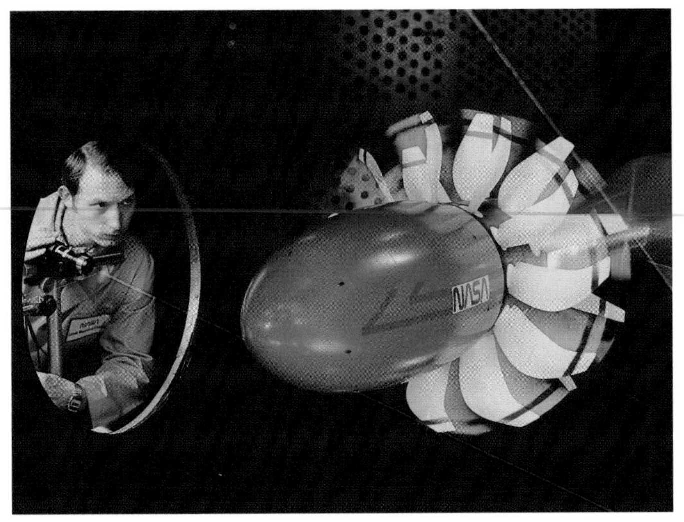

Normal beams of light spread out, but laser beams stay narrow.

How a laser is used

Laser beams can carry TV and radio signals to people's homes. The signals are very powerful and can be sent a long way through cables.

CD players also use a laser beam. The beam shines on to the CD. The pattern of light which is reflected is the code for the music. Nothing actually touches the disc, so it doesn't wear out. Doctors use lasers to cut like knives during operations. Laser beams can also burn away tumours.

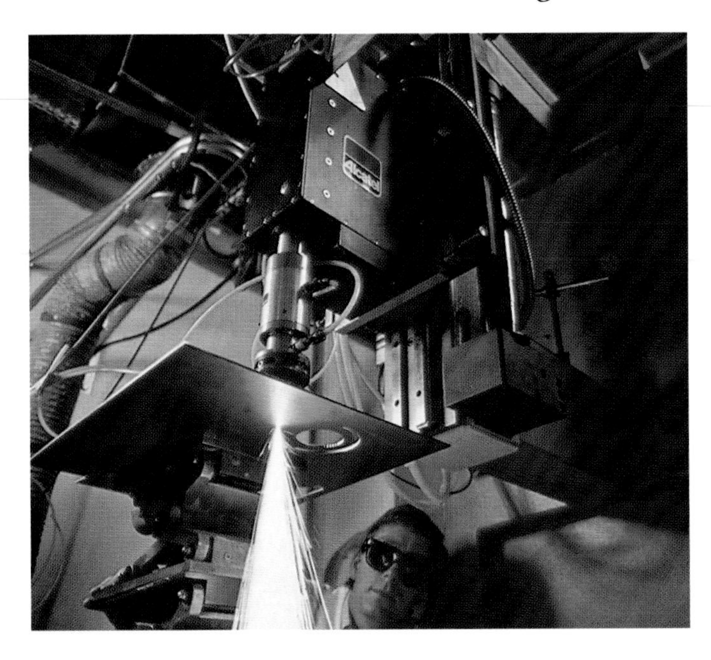

This laser machine is being held by a robot arm. The arm moves along and shoots out laser beams to cut cleanly through the metal.

Leaf

See also: Photosynthesis, Plant

A leaf is the part of a plant which makes the plant's food. Green plants grow almost everywhere, except where it is very cold or very dry. Different plants have different-shaped leaves.

Life of a leaf

A leaf grows from a bud which forms on the stem. The bud opens and a new leaf and stem begin to grow. The leaves of some plants live for years but the leaves of many others wither and die after several months.

People and animals could not live without leaves. Many animals feed on the leaves of grass and other plants. Meat-eaters feed on plant-eating animals. People eat the leaves of some plants and use others as medicines. Tea is made from the leaves of tea plants.

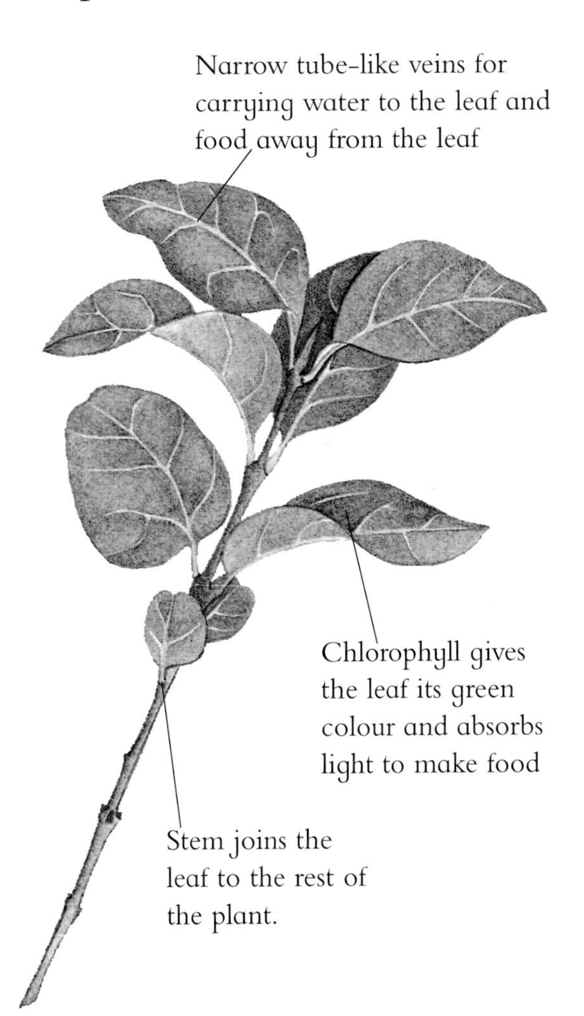

The African raffia palm has the largest leaves of any tree. They grow up to 20 m long.

DID YOU KNOW?

Some leaves change colour in the autumn before they fall off the trees and plants. This is because the water supply to the leaves has been cut stopping green chlorophyll from forming.

Lebanon

See also: Asia

Lebanon is a country in the Middle East. It has two mountain ranges. Between them there is good land for growing crops. There is a narrow coast in the west. Summers are hot. Winters are cool, with some rain.

Beirut has a natural harbour that has been used by ships for thousands of years.

Living and working

Most people in Lebanon live in the cities and towns. There are some industries that make things from chemicals, gold and silver. In the good farming area, farmers grow fruits, olives, grapes and tobacco. Olives are very popular as a snack in Lebanon.

People have been living in Lebanon for thousands of years. In recent times, Lebanon has suffered nearly 50 years of war in the fighting between Arabs, Palestinians and Israelis.

DID YOU KNOW?

The tree called the Cedar of Lebanon has been a symbol of the country for at least 2000 years. It is on Lebanon's flag. Some Cedars of Lebanon are over 3000 years old.

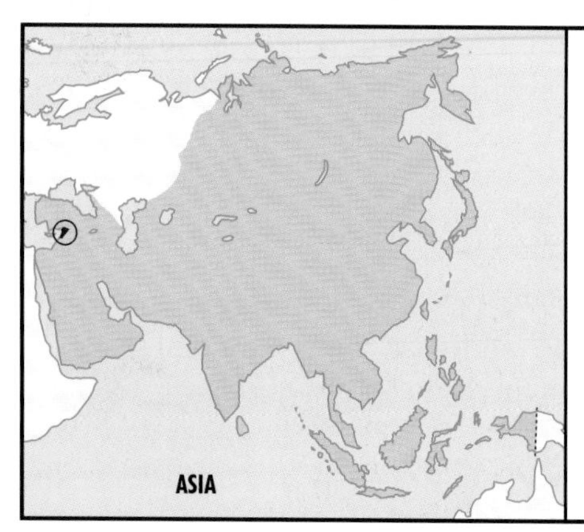

FACT FILE

PEOPLE	Lebanese
POPULATION	2.9 million
MAIN LANGUAGES	Arabic, French
CAPITAL CITY	Beirut
MONEY	Lebanese pound
HIGHEST MOUNTAIN	Qurnat as Sawdā' – 3088 m
LONGEST RIVER	River Litani – 145 km

Legend

See also: Literature, Myth, Story

A legend is a story which has been handed down through many generations. The story is often about heroes or exciting events. Legends can have magical or supernatural things in them, but they are always about human beings. This makes them different from myths which are about gods or supernatural beings. Every country in the world has its own legends.

John Chapman, known as Johnny Appleseed, was a real man.

Real and pretend

Many legends may be based on real people. For example, the English legends of King Arthur may have been about a real person. But the legend also says that he had a magic sword called Excalibur, a magician called Merlin and that he sat his knights at a round table. Some of these things may have been added to the story as it was retold again and again.

Johnny Appleseed

Johnny Appleseed was the nickname of an American settler of the 1800s. His real name was John Chapman. Because he planted apple trees, people called him Appleseed. Even though he was a real person, many of the stories about him and his family are made up. He has now become the hero of legends.

This picture showing King Arthur and his knights is 600 years old.

Leopard

See also: Cat, Mammal

The leopard is a member of the cat family. It is a mammal. Leopards live across Africa and southern Asia. Most live on the grassy plains, but leopards can live in very hot areas and high up mountains.

LEOPARD FACTS

NUMBER OF KINDS....7
COLOUR.....yellow with black and brown spots, or totally black
LENGTH..... up to 190 cm
HEIGHT...... up to 8 cm
WEIGHT..... up to 90 kg
STATUS....... endangered
LIFE SPAN... about 12 years
ENEMIES..... people

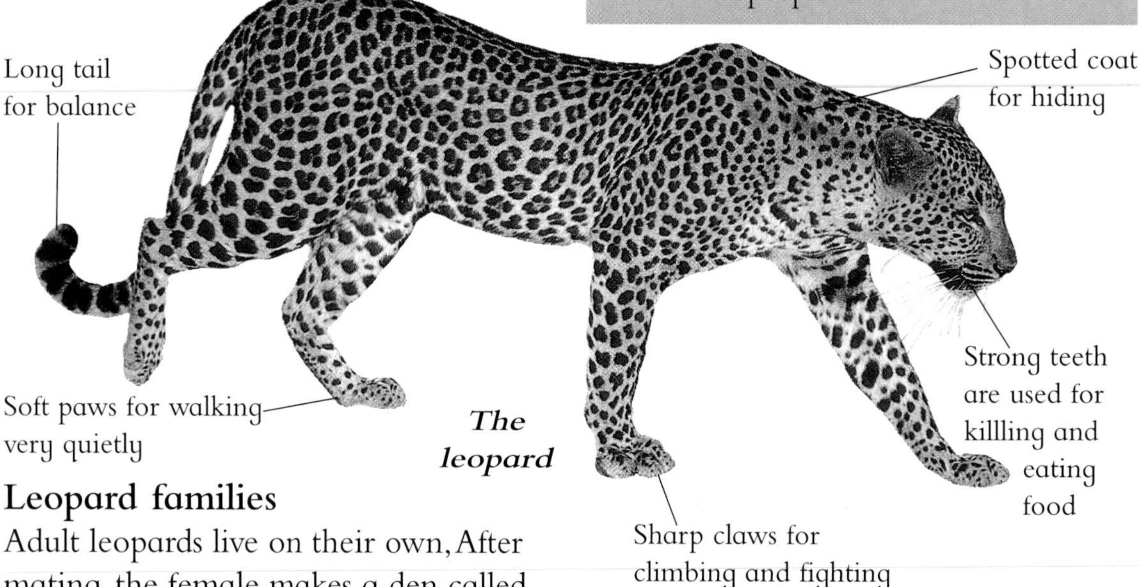

The leopard

Leopard families

Adult leopards live on their own, After mating, the female makes a den called a lair, where she has her babies, called cubs. They stay with their mother for about two years. When the cubs are very small, the mother moves her lair every few days for safety.

FOOD

A leopard likes to catch antelopes, baboons and warthogs, but will also eat smaller animals and birds. The leopard carries its food up into trees out of reach of lions and vultures.

A female leopard with her cub.